SO SPECIAL

I feel ridiculous with my inner child
So girly maybe, I might take me out like I'd do with her
So special baby, special K, need a date?
Ladies Not Today
I am going out alone
I am in my zone, I can bone alone
This master's baited, I mean I got a babe
She might rather I not say it
But it slipped, cat didn't get my tongue
On that oral shit, eat food, movies and lay back in the crib
"You such a kid"
But I'm all grown-up, kidding with me like a baby now
I feel the cloud, of gloominess feel comforting now
A safe tavern, my mind feels like a perfect place to just recline
Minding mines, but I got a sensory antenna that's always up
I sense it, don't be fooled by my misplaced foolery
I don't clamor to bull, shit
I will slay your ass, leave y'all in a funk for dissing sake
A big mistake taking my quiet demeanor for weakness

DREAMERZ Featuring JOE BUDDEN

{Verse 1: Chiggy}

I quit daydreaming, dreaming awake now
Barely sleeping, only dreams I got were the sleepy ones
But I don't feel battered up, I got her feet back up
Oh silly me, I got my feet down, she backs me up
No dream girls, it feels real now
I would thought she'd go for a husband but she's "Miss Right Now."
I piped down, no more crazy stunts on that love shit
It feels comfortable, I'm hospitable
Me seeming lame ain't even possible
But I'd act lame now just to fuck with you
"So not cool you acting now," and then, she pouts
"Be real, are we really going out?"
Let's just chill, no need to label it, but I want the south
I mean the cat, but she is really cool with the things I be about

[Verse 2: Joe Budden]
Check it,
More questions, more answers
More c_i smoke and more cancer
More arguing, more resistance
Its seems like the closer we get, its more distance
More angles, a million different looks
Was on the same page, just in different books
there's so much i want to say but i got no ground
cause we ain't break up, more like broke down
now that's pain and torture
add that with restraining orders
then add the soul of my slain daughter
none of this is how we planned it to be
one big insanity plea
shit could never end amicably
I miss you trying
you probably think don't think I try too
when you stubborn and prideful
not much is insightful
but God was trying to show me something
He ain't think that I knew
sometimes shit that doesn't breathe can die too

[Hook: Emanny]
Were we just dreamerz?
Waiting for our shot to shoot to the moon
Were we just dreamerz?
Spending our lives trying to see this thing through
Waiting to fly away
Waiting to fly away
Waiting to fly away
waiting to fly away

[Verse 3: Joe Budden]
How we go from thoughts of marriage
Thoughts of me copping carrots
Talks of what we'd name her while shopping for a carriage
But when the dream stopped, who knew you'd see me like a savage
That you dreamt of vacations, but only woke up with baggage
All you ever did was love me, and look at where it got you
And when you wanted more, all I did was say I'm not you
I'm selfish not selfless, and I say that with love
so in essence you're asking for what I'm incapable of
so now I find I'm going over choices I ain't even made yet
were we clouded by good times of great sex?

running fast towards an unknown fate
that altered when I introduced you to my unknown traits
in your dreams, seems you had me pegged as another man
but in mine, only you would understand
in our minds we were perfect
we witnessed our dream get murdered
now reality is on trial and we both awaiting the verdict

[Bridge 1: Joe Budden]
But you'll always be close to me
though you said this ain't how it's supposed to be
what we had was so real
but you said I don't care
never thought this day would come
you said you gave your all and was left with none
but we can both be spared
but you don't think that's fair, that's fair

[Hook]

[Verse 4: Joe Budden]
You can't see how you ever began to like a liar
you lost track of all the little things that I admired
but when the peace left, I knew we might retire
thinking man, I live upstairs, I'm something like somaya
got memories, but at what point are they lost
you say we could work through it, at what point is it forced?
we shoulda never rushed
cause it's like now we at a point where you won't never trust
and for me I can't believe that's all we ever was
the high's gone, need a better buzz
Cause we sleep in the same bed, but we never touch
my solution to every beef is to revisit
though we'll have the same emotions we won't be so livid
won't be so vivid
I think your girl secretly applauded our drama
we don't need those critics
we owe it to go over our foundation with a keen eye
sad part to say you never have the same dream twice

[Bridge 2: Emanny]
We let love and all its possibility
take us from reality
made it hard to see that
we were bound together
just to cover up the pain

I'm wishing the skies were rain
and wipe all my thoughts away
cause I'm tired of dreaming

ALWAYS TWISTED Featuring TREY SONGZ

[CHIGGY]

I feel really funky when I hear ya songz
Ladies stay bitchin', holla at me, Dog
This Boy so crazy, maybe
Reason I ain't having that, girl, is cause you so wack
Get back, retract ya ass
Lame asses, I mean y'all better haul ass
Ain't on that lame shit
Baby, everything I got, I own it
Broke, but money talking crazy like it's lost it
I mean I'm cool with my low cash
Bad Boy, go on Chiggy with your mad ass
Crazy-ass Bastard
With my eyes on baby with her fat ass
The way she's sittin' down , everybody can spot her ass crack
Backpack rappers ain't even finding that funny no more
Way I make these corny raps feel like dope lyrical facts

[Chiggy's CHORUS]

I am always twisted when I hit the clubs
Pockets fulla lints, but girls fuck with the boy
Ladies gimme dap, Em shows me love
But on that Huggie shit, girl, pamper ya boy!

[TREY SONGZ]

Always twisted
When I leave the club
Body full of liquor
Playing with ya girl
And since I'm Trey
You know she loving me
Tell her I love her back
And when she done with me
You can have her back (ready?)
Songz let 'em know bout the day

August 4th, Ready on the way
Black tint on the whip
While the driver driving
Hottest motherfucker in the world inside it
And while you the world residing
I'm on another planet
Haters internet spam him
They can't stand him
Trey say damn them
Tell em leave the turkey brother cause I'm bout to ham them
Tre maine spit flames
Can somebody bring the fans in
Better yet the hoes in
Tell em leave their clothes in the bin at the front door
What I gotta front for
Flow so graphic
With the beat and plastic
Wrap it
Throw it in the dirt
Dig it up
All you niggas dirt
Give it up
Big whip, big wheels
When I pop like jurassic
Skinny girls and chicks with thick asses
See green like the masters
Tiger when I bite her
Stick my wood up inside her
She ignite my fire
Treat me like a pacifier
Hope she don't burn through the rubber like the tires
When I'm? in the chevy
Like I'm driving it for hire
(Whoaaa, and she know)
I'm always twisted
When I leave the club
Body full of liquid
Pockets full of dubs
Heading to the telly or to another club
Tell me is you ready
You want me to beat it up
Beat it up, beat it up
Baby is you keeping up
Got the money
Got the fame
But to me that ain't enough

Ain't the type to complain
I just beat a nigga up
You niggas get out my lane
Watch my feet and keep my dust
They always bitching
When I'm in the club
Cause all they bitches
Wanna give it up
VIP cause she like what she sees
And the bottles on me
Soo the bottles are free for her
She wanna see me with her
I wanna see me her and her friend
Doing it again and again and again
Shorty gonna spin
Quick don't let it slip
When you keep the dick in
Girl you know you know I'm so nasty
And I won't let your fat ass walk pass mee
I wanna rub your body down like you are ashy
Call a nigga lasie
Do anything you ask me
Shorty give that mega brain, mega brain
So insane
Long as you don't paper plane
Government tax me
Actually
I'm golden shit
You can go hold this shit

COLD WIND BLOWS Featuring Eminem

[Intro]
Cause some things just don't change
It's better when they stay the same
Although the whole world knows your name
So on a bigger stage they came to see you spit your game
Ooooohhhhhhh
It shouldn't be difficult to explain
Just why you came back again, you hate the fame
Love the game, cold as ice you remain
Fuck em' all, tell 'em all eat shit, here we go again

So, god damn... is it that time again already
Haha, you don't look too happy to see me

Fuck man, don't everybody welcome me back at once
All right, fuck ya'll then

{Chiggy}

I'm onto big fish, got mad bitches, on my stick
They ride with joy, now call it my joystick
My bitches swing both ways
So spoilt or should I say, rotten like tooth decay
I slay, bitches, got them needing, stitches
to patch they pussies up
Be scared cats cause I rip pussies
Fuck google, I make a bitch goggle
Slurped it up, baby, don't you dare fumble
It's only cum...sip a little rum....use lubricant
Go ahead cunt, why you dey front?
You know you want it
That's the way you like it
Don't bite it, don't fight it, just slide it
Ride it like a Merry, let your pussy Go-Round, as you grind it

Cause baby, nobody wanna hear nice shit no mo'
That's why I'm nasty when I Flow

[Eminem]
You can get the dick, just call me the ballsack, I'm nuts
Michael Vick in this bitch, dog fall back you mutts
Fuck your worms, you never seen such a sick puppy
Fuck it a sick duck, I want my duck sick mummy
And my nuts, licked, gobble 'em up trick, yummy
Bitch you don't fucking think I know that you suck dick dummy?
You'll get your butt kicked, fuck all that love shit honey
Yeah I laugh when I call you a slut, it's funny!
Shawty dance while I diss you to the beat, fuck the words
You don't listen to 'em anyway, yeah struck a nerve sucker
Motherfucker might as well let my lips pucker
Like Elton John, cause I'm just a mean cock sucker
This shit is on, cause you went and pissed me off
Now I'm shitting and pissing on everybody
Give a fuck if it's right or wrong
So buck the Buddha, light a bong
But take a look at mariah the next time I inspire you to write a song, c'mon

[Chorus]
Oh oh oh oh oh oh oh, I'm as cold as the cold wind blows
When it snows and it's twenty be-low
Ask me why man I just don't know know know know know know know

I'm as cold as the cold wind blows blo-blo-blo-blo-blo-blows
Oh oh oh oh oh

[Eminem]
Fuck it I'm a loose cannon, Bruce Banner's back in the booth
Ya'll are sitting ducks, I'm the only goose standing
I set the world on fire, piss on it, put it out
Stick my dick in a circle, but I'm not fucking around motherfucker
I'll show you pussy footin, I'll kick a bitch in the cunt
'Til it makes her queef and sounds like a fucking whoopy cushion
Who the fuck is you pushin', you musta mistook me for some sissy
Soft punk looking for some nookie or bosom
Go ahead, fucking hater push me
I told you ain't no fucking way to shush me
Call me a faggot cause I hate a pussy
Man the fuck up sissy, G's up
All you gardeners freeze up, put your hoes down (shady ease up!)
Man chill, nah I can't god damnit
Rap is a landfill, drop the anvil
These are shoes that you can't fill
Shit the day that happens the world'll stop spinning
And Michael J. Fox'll come to a stand still
During an earthquake, urine in your face
Cause you're fake, ahh what the fuck, that hurt wait!
Ahh what the fuck, I just got struck by lightening
Alright then I quit, god I give up
Call it evil that men do, lord forgive me for what my pen do
This is for your sins, I cleanse you
You can repent but I warn you, if you continue
To hell I'll send you, and just then the wind blew and I said

Oh oh oh oh oh oh oh, I'm as cold as the cold wind blows
When it snows and it's twenty be-low
Ask me why man I just don't know know know know know know know
I'm as cold as the cold wind blows blo-blo-blo-blo-blo-blows
Oh oh oh oh oh

[Eminem]
How long will I be this way? Shady until my dying day
'Til I hang up the mic and it's time for me to say
So long, 'til then I drop the fucking bombs
Like I miss the pass when I went long
If you don't like it you can kiss my ass in a lint thong
Now sing along, slut this, slut that, learn the words to the song
Oh bitches don't like that, homie I'll be nicer to women
When the aqua man drowns and the human torch starts swimming

Man I'm a cold soul, I roll solo so
So don't compare me to them other bums over there
It's like apples to oranges, peaches to plums yeah
I'm bananas pussy, cut off the grapes and grow a pair
But I swear, you try to diss me, I'll slaughter you
I put that on everything, like everyone does with auto-tune
That last thing you wanna do is have me spit out a rhyme
And say I was writing this and I thought of you so

Oh oh oh oh oh oh oh, I'm as cold as the cold wind blows
When it snows and it's twenty be-low
Ask me why man I just don't know know know know know know know
I'm as cold as the cold wind blows blo-blo-blo-blo-blo-blo-blows
Oh oh oh oh oh

[Outro]
Oh oh oh oh oh oh
I don't know, I don't know what caused, I don't know what caused me to be this way
I don't know, I don't know but I probably be this way 'til my dying day
I don't know why I'm so, I'm so cold mean things I don't mean to say
I guess this is how you made me

THERE GOES MY BABY Featuring Usher

{Chiggy}

On my LL Cool J shit
Sexy, Crazy and so Cool
Rewind with me baby
Memories of when I was back in High School
Feeling shorty, but too awkward to sway her focus on me
But, butt with a butt like Jlo's
How can I falter, and be lackadaisical with how I feel for ya
So persistent
Insisting on Joe Budden's old girl, Somaya
Rihanna's fine ass wanted by me, Dead Or Alive
Dead her ass, back shots erotically make me cum, alive!
But I'm gunnin' for the long haul
U-haul so sexy when she backs me up against the wall
Grindin', dirty whining
Reclined way back like a lazy boy
A manly boy that's Knee-deep into Freud
Sike-Chology, Yaris, I want an Orgy
My dick feels turgid, nicki gimme the nicki
I mean I want a kiss, nicki

Today I feel really freaky
Must be Friday, I could swear on my pinky!

{Usher}

There goes my baby
(oo girl look at you)
You don't know how good it feels to call you my girl
There goes my baby
Loving everything you do
Oo girl look at you

Bet you ain't know that I be checking you out
When you be putting your heels on
I swear your body's so perfect baby
How you work it baby yea
I love the way that you be poking it out
Girl give me something to feel on
So please believe we gone be twerking it out
By the end of the night baby

I've been waiting all day to wrap my hands
Around your waist and kiss your face
Wouldn't trade this feeling for nothing
Not even for a minute
And I'll sit here long as it takes
To get you all alone
But as soon as you come walking my way
You gon hear me say

There goes my baby
(oo girl look at you)
You don't know how good it feels to call you my girl
There goes my baby
Loving everything you do
Oo girl look at you

I get the chills whenever I see your face
And you in the place girl
Feel like I'm in a movie baby
I'm like oowee baby oh
Like waterfalls your hair falls down to your waist
Can I get a taste girl
No need to keep this baby
I ain't ashamed of calling your name girl

I've been waiting all day to wrap my hands
Around your waist and kiss your face

Wouldn't trade this feeling for nothing
Not even for a minute
And I'll sit here long as it takes
To get you all alone
But as soon as you come walking my way
You gon hear me say

There goes my baby
(oo girl look at you)
You don't know how good it feels to call you my girl
There goes my baby
Loving everything you do
Oo girl look at you

And girl I feel like it's our first time
Everytime we get together
Baby loving you feels better than
Everything, anything
Put on my heart you don't need a ring
And I promise our time away won't change my love

There goes my baby
(oo girl look at you)
You don't know how good it feels to call you my girl
There goes my baby
Loving everything you do
Oo girl look at you

There goes my baby
(oo girl look at you)
You don't know how good it feels to call you my girl
There goes my baby
Loving everything you do
Oo girl look at you

THE KISS (SKIT)

I'm gonna kill this bitch
I'm a kill him
I'm going to fuckin' jail
'Cuz I'm gonna kill this bitch
Yo man
What?
I don't know
I gotta really, really bad feelin' about this

Man would you shut the fuck up
You always gotta bad feelin' man
That's her car right there
Aight let me park
Just park
I'm parkin'
Fuckin', turn the car off dog
Aight
Aight we wait
We wait for what?
We wait until she comes out
And then I'm gonna fuckin' kill her
Man, you ain't gonna kill no one
What the fuck did you bring that for?
Man shut the fuck up dog
Just shut up, the fuckin' clip is empty
Man, don't point that shit at me
It's not even loaded bitch, look
Dude, God I fuckin' hate it when you do that shit
Yea, but it's funny as fuck
Muthafucka I'm gonna kill you
One of these days, I swear
Gets you every time
Is that her?
Where?
Right there mothafucka
Ooh, yeah
Aight get down, get down
Fuck, what you doing to her?
Get down
What the fuck you want me to get under the car?
Yo, who she walkin' with?
How the fuck am I suppose to know?
You told me to duck down
It's the fuckin' bouncer
Did she just kiss him?
I don't think so
Dog, she just fuckin' kissed him
No she didn't
She's kissin' him dog
No she's not
Oh shit
Come on
Mutherfucker
No

NBA (Never Broke Again) Featuring Joe Budden

[Hook:]
Bitch I'm ballin', bitch I'm ballin'
Racked up, no wallet
Keep a bad bitch in my team
I should join the league
NBA, never broke again, never going broke again
NBA, never broke again, never going broke again
Cause bitch I'm ballin', bitch I'm ballin
I fuck her once, don't call her
My niggas gettin' that green, we in a different league
NBA, never broke again, never going broke again
NBA, never broke again, never going broke again

{Verse 1: Chiggy}

If Money Could Talk

I'm sensual yet sexual
So in tune with my body parts, and dick
Dictating what my precedents or standards be
I'm sick, with no dead presidents
But I got a roll of nickels and of quarters buried in the backyard
I'ma get hard on the girls
If she provokin' my hard-on
Money tree growing ever so timidly
I'm bullshit, now chicago best walk with me
Or duck quickly as I begin to talk that shit
Money talks but chigozie is more fluent, B!
A roll of Honor student
I got a role so play y'alls bitches
I regressed back into a relapse
And freestyled Marshall Mathers near distant lyrics
A rich spirit, who broke Amanda Bynes' critics
Hearts cause I felt she was crazy enough to be in my group's kitchen (key chain?)
You smell what Joey, or Emmy or Chiggy be busy cooking?
The 'Nsane Asylum go get y'all mind right, bitches

BULLSHIT walking and talking
I guess I must be balling
With the Basketball team with Mr. Air Jordan
Stalling, never that
Calling? Girl I fucked telepathically
Her body needs a hard poking
Nigga, your bitch is damn open!

[Verse 2: Joe Budden]

Talkin' money but walkin' funny, is it any reason ya'll starvin'
I spell bull and by spelling force
Do I really need to bag your part?
And my jersey say James I don't play games,
Like Bron when he in that Garden
And, wait I said that all wrong,
She don't need to rock when I put my hard in
My new nickname is just watch
Might not join might just watch
New yacht master just a watch
Doubten me I tell em just watch
Them diamonds yellow them beams are red
And them hands are tucked they don't show
Plus them shooters with me got the green light
So why the fuck you don't think they won't go?
Hold up, your chick traded post game
And no shame she felt your man
She probably on Joe Johnson
Cause I never be on that Elton Brand
It's YSL, she's fly as hell
Tell the come to go to my ride
You can't blame hoes ain't Peter Rose
Now she a thorne in my side
Grow up, P-R-P-S is over my Timbs
Way shorty blew me at it was only right I showed her my bench
Let my millions hit, when the fan hit
Spend all these bills on liquor
Fricken Jersey love is team
Still we got the realest niggas Joey

{Hook}:

(Verse 3: Chiggy}

Still The Man

If you could bullshit me
I'd probably be a much more satisfied customer
Consumer or lover
Smashing a lot of girls waiting for a train running southwards
I'm east-bound, tryna pick up Joey by the Turn pike
With an ill spiked hair, looking like Kayla Garcia with her mohawk derriere
+NO AIR+ plays

I'm really rocking a crew cut fade
(Got lucky?) No luck, babe
I got a burden now feeling like I need Joe Budden's last name
Chigozie Budden
The Nigerian Joe Budden
Emcees can no longer breathe freely
Since I'm zenith solely on my lyrical position
They're locked up or trapped in my lyrical pri-son with crappy conditions
As far as me dissing, I'm void of competitors
Radio static'fied with bullshit frequently
I'm still the man to exercise decency
My songs are hushed on radio, but go online you can hear them yo!

{Hook}:

GOTHIC GYPSY

Spiritually mystical, shit coulda got critical
But for real, I call it a spade, baby, bury hatchets now
Wound up now, past medical
Medically I'm okay, pal
Just a little off, mental how?
Possible is it that if I'm yet so logical
Dumb it down for the crowd
But Joe, forgiving the naysayers and bullshitters
ain't what my plans be about
I wanna see 'em stew in the mess they was tryna see me in
Little thing is people's worry ain't my worry now
Money is the root to my lust
I can't be married to them, but nigerian girls do get it now
I'ma look at you ridiculous like I see P. Diddy thinking I'm a low-life
Cause I am all over twitter now

The gypsy, is tipsy
One more drink from my baby's body, I need, B
I am tipsy

So you sweat me to like you
But as if I wasn't in the same old shoes,
I find you unlikely
To be for real, baby
Get some shades for how bright I think, B
Cause mentally, I shine, not sure you might get embrigtened
Not likely, but stay enlightened on the progress I've made, B

Weather my weather, storm off if I piss you off
But you feel greater cause your dough stacks higher
But mentally rigid with mines, I'm richer
Spiritually distinguished,
Sidekick soraya, my mini-me midget
I'ma sic her ass on y'all like honey go get 'em, cats
Pussyfooting around the idea of love reaching its fullstop
Fool stop
Get it right, I am so far gone
But the old lady I liked as a kid is with whom I am so far done.

The Gypsy, is typsy
One more drink from my baby's body, I need, B
I am tipsy

So somaya, where did we stop?
I forgot about you a while ago, should I let go
And just roll with my better side or have y'all as better halves
Divided my attention between both two girls
But more girls are seeking for this lover's attention
Call it love, call it sex, but really it's lustful
And lost, fool on deaf ears
Reason people need a duster to dust up on the stale news
I figured what I need or want long before she gave in
But I got upset feeling she thought I was planning without her Opinion as add-ons, but it made me tear up like onions
Sorry soraya, but believe me
When I say I am hell-bent on providing soul-wise
Or mentally for ya
Sex ain't all it's all bout
But a physical love I crave now more than ever
'Else I be a phone buddy like I was to the others (girls, that is)

The Gypsy, is tipsy
On more drink from my baby's body, I need, B
I am tipsy

INFINITE Featuring Eminem

{Verse 1: Chiggy}
I'm Infinite
Y'all heard of hell, Chiggy has been to it
Back with a vengeance, there ain't no cents in it
I mean no sense in me rhyming commercially
But I'd go plati-num if I was Eminem
Lyrically on that level

But realistically, my cult followers are minimal
So critical and cynical
I'm sick, and there's no drugs available
Christ, milfs do turn me on
I wanna be inside ya mom like a baby
Deep in her cunt with my right now throbbing hard-on
Shady baby, she's a shaken lady
So surprised by my acts and no longer knows how to react
Cautious maybe, reason I don't feel like I'm 'Nsane
Is cause I make so much sense when I talk crazy
Y'all fugazi, Chigozie Ugwueze's so Mr. Right
I'm so right about my take on things
I'm Crass Silly and Morbid Funny
Retardedly humorous, a hole and a donkey
An Asshole
Fags know, not to test me anally
I'm more annoying (so anal)
Dispensing my thoughts to Joey like two co-joined twins!
The Yin and his Yang
I'm Jin with how I make these lyrics go bang!

[Verse 2: Eminem]
Ayo, my pen and paper cause a chain reaction
To get your brain relaxing, a zany acting maniac in action
A brainiac in fact son, you mainly lack attraction
You look insanely whack when just a fraction of my tracks run
My rhyming skills got you climbing hills
I travel through your mind into your spine like siren drills
I'm sliming grills of roaches, with sprayed on disinfectants
Twist the necks of rappers 'til their spinal column disconnects
We disinfect then check the monologue, turn your system up
Twist them up, and indulge in the marijuana smog
This is the season for noise pollution contamination
Examination of more cartoons than animation
My lamination of narration
Hit's a snare and bass of track fucked up rapper interrogation
When I declare invasion, there ain't no time to be stare and gazing
I turn the stage into a barren wasteland...
I'm Infinite

[Chorus:]
You heard of hell well I was sent from it
I went to it serving a sentence for murderin' instruments
Now I'm trying to repent from it
But when I hear the beat I'm tempted to make another attempt at it...
I'm Infinite

[Verse 3: Eminem]
Bust it, I let the beat commence so I can beat the sense of your elite defense
I got some meat to mince, a crew to stomp and two feet to rinse
I greet the gents and ladies, I spoil loyal fans
I foil plans and leave fluids leaking like oil pans
My coil hands around this microphone are lethal
One thought in my cerebral is deeper then a Jeep full of people
MC's are feeble, I came to cause some pandemonium
Battle a band of phony MC's and stand the lonely one
Imitator, Intimidator, Stimulator, Simulator of data, Eliminator
There's never been a greater since the burial of Jesus
Fuck around and catch all of the venereal diseases
My thesis will smash a stereo to pieces
My accapella releases classic masterpieces through telekinesis
And eases you mentally, gently, sentimentally, instrumentally
With entity, dementedly meant to be Infinite

[Chorus:]
You heard of hell well I was sent from it
I went to it serving a sentence for murderin' instruments
Now I'm trying to repent from it
But when I hear the beat I'm tempted to make another attempt at it...
I'm Infinite

[Verse 4: Eminem]
Man I got evidence I'm never dense and I been clever ever since
My residence was hesitant to do some shit that represents the M-O
So I'm assuming all responsibility
Cause there's a monster will in me that always wants to kill MC's
Mic messaler, slamming like a wrestler
Here to make a mess of a lyric smuggling embezzler
No one is specialer, My skill is intergalactical
I get cynical act a fool then I send a crew back to school
I never packed a tool or acted cool, it wasn't practical
I'd rather let a tactical, tact full track tickle your fancy
In fact I can't see, or can't imagine
A man who ain't a lover of beats or a fan of scratching
This is for my family, the kid who had a cameo on my last jam
Plus the man who never had a plan B
Be all you can be, cause once you make an instant hit
I'm tensed a bit and tempted when I see the sins my friends commit...
I'm Infinite

[Chorus:]
You heard of hell well I was sent from it
I went to it serving a sentence for murderin' instruments
Now I'm trying to repent from it
But when I hear the beat I'm tempted to make another attempt at it...

I'm Infinite
You heard of hell well I was sent from it
I went to it serving a sentence for murderin' instruments
Now I'm trying to repent from it
But when I hear the beat I'm tempted to make another attempt at it...
I'm Infinite

::::BONUS::::

NICKELS NO DIMES (SKIT)

Drugs and Bitches
I pop pills, I drop dimes
I drop her lame ass if it ain't acting right
I got right, now gimme change
Nickels No Dimes
Y'all make me feel strange

"Love without money ain't possible
I can't buy her love, I ain't rich enough
But I ain't distraught nor do I feel lame!
But then again, she's out of my league
I mean, Baby girl ain't EVEN on my league
I GOT nickels...LOOSE change...BUTT, she's so DIME!

THROW THAT (SLAUGHTERHOUSE Featuring Chiggy)

[Eminem - Hook]
She strips, to get tips
Those lips and those childbearing hips
I'll throw this, I'll throw this dick on you girl (girl)
I'll throw this, I'll throw this dick on you girl (girl)

Gonna make you feel me, gonna shake this building till I make you spill drinks
Girl, this whole building is probably filled with little dingalings
But not me, I- I throw this dick on you girl
I throw this, I throw this dick on you girl

[Royce Da 5'9"]
They call me Nickel Nina aka (ROYCE!) aka (throw dat dick?)
A player gotta keep a condom on cause we play safe
Eh, then I'm taking the condom off cause I skeet they face
Then I turn off Jodeci cause they say "baby want you to stay but you can't stay"

It ain't trickin' it if you gettin it, if you ain't got that you ain't ballin'
You mad, they call me botox up in Hermes cause I help them get rid of all those bags
(All those bags) I throw this brick on you girl
Then I drink up, whats your number?
I'ma throw this dick on you girl

She's got it, ohhh she got all the homies in here
Excited, ohh I don't really know how to describe it

The strippers love me and I love them too
My bitch gon be like what am I gon do witchu

[Eminem - Hook]

[Crooked I]
I'm Crooked I, aka fuck your girl
Up up in the sky
When it come down, say "FUCK THE WOOOORLD"
These strippers are sprung
My middle initial is awful richard and my nicknames
right on the tip of her tongue
The side of her mouth is dripping with (EH, eh-eh)
I'm drunk right now, stomped right now
Tryna figure out how to get four chicks to sit on one chair
Oh yeah, turn the chair upside down, upside down
I throw this grip on you girl
Talking that handcuff you ain't never coming home
Man finna trip on your girl

She's got it, ohhh she got all the homies in here
Excited, ohhh, I don't really know how to describe it

Baby you got some incredible skills
I want brain you want shoes
True love's always head over heels

[Eminem - Hook]

[Bridge]
I said yo yo
You got me on the string I'm dangling like a yoyo
You string me along and leave me hanging and thats a NO No
In my world, cause I throw this thing on you girl

[Joe Budden]
Look, they call me Joe Butt-in
I be around when them hoes strut in
This relationship is 50/50

If you meet me halfway I get the whole nut in
Cause I'm in town, just one day now spin round
Get ya face out the way
And just when she want an encore, I'm gone
I'm sorry I couldn't stay

[Chiggy]
My name Is
They call me Chiggy
But y'all knew that has always been me
Slaughtering cowards who too shook to contend
Lyrically, peep the way I fuck with mics
Woo mics, serenading
Mic checks bouncing on y'all
Y'all too broke lyrically no wonder y'all ain't good at emceeing
I stay seeing that dead folks
Ain't worth worrying about
Niggaz acting like spirits on that mic, shit!
They floatin' about the game
I stay buoyant, get ya floaters, niggaz
Y'all won't last
Everlast, whitey Ford on y'all bitch asses
Dog Butts, If I was rich I'ma date Escorts
Hookers, strippers and Pros at suctions
Y'all suck, cuz
Get lust or get busted when this "Dick" erupts
I vent like a volcano
Flush y'all down the drains like Draino
Baby Jlo riding with me
How sick is y'all niggaz?
Chiggy's sickness lyrically is too unreal!
I'm so so real (Surreal)!

[Joell Ortiz]
They call me O-E double-L Ortiz
AKA Yaowa, aka ah nuttin, I just got an ak in my jeans
Can I spray your flower
I ain't really tryna sit with you girl
When you finish that spit lets split
Wheres your wrist let me throw this grip on you girl

She's got it, ohhh she got all the homies in here excited,
ohhh, I don't really know how to describe it

...before this night is a blur, here's my offer
That shit you did, do that with her
And both of you girls..?

[Eminem - Hook]
(Throw dat dick)

BLACK AND YELLOW (Wiz Khalifa Featuring Chiggy)

(Chiggy's rap}

I'm back in this bitch
Oradult y'all, we all up in this bitch
You can smell that we the shit
Cause Sauit Bora, Sauit Bora
Got the ladies in stilettos
Wanna grab ahold a fellow
Popping they booty on the flo'
Dip it low, pick it up slow
This is Christmas and it's cold
Fuck ya coat cause we turning winter to a scalding show
You ain't ready
We blowing this town to confetti
Leaving Debris in the aftermath
We so on crack and y'all so wack
You don't deserve the crown, make do with the cap
We killing it this year, coming through like fear
That the end of y'all's era is near!

{Wiz Khalifa}

Yeah, uh huh, you know what it is
Black and yellow [x4]
Yeah, uh huh, you know what it is
Black and yellow [x4]

[Chorus:]
Yeah, uh huh, you know what it is
Everything I do, I do it big
Yeah, uh huh, screaming that's nothing
What I pulled off the lot, that's stunting
Repping my town when you see me you know everything
Black and yellow [x4]
I put it down from the whip to my diamonds, I'm in
Black and yellow [x4]

[Verse 1:]
Black stripe, yellow paint, them niggas scared of it but them hoes ain't
Soon as I hit the club look at them hoes face
Hit the pedal once make the floor shake
Suede inside, my engine roaring
It's the big boy, you know what I payed for it
And I got the pedal to the metal
I got you niggas checking game I'm balling out on every level
Hear them haters talk but there's nothing you can tell 'em
Just made a million, got another million on my schedule
No love for 'em nigga breaking hearts
No keys, push to start

[Chorus:]
Yeah, uh huh, you know what it is
Everything I do, I do it big
Yeah, uh huh screaming that's nothing
What I pulled off the lot, that's stunting
Repping my town when you see me you know everything
Black and yellow [x4]
I put it down from the whip to my diamonds I'm in
Black and yellow [x4]

[Verse 2:]
Got a call from my jeweler, this just in
Bitches love me 'cause I'm fucking with their best friends
Not a lesbian but she a freak though
This ain't for one night I'm shining all weak hoe.
I'm sipping cleeko and rocking yellow diamonds
So many rocks up in the watch I cant tell what the time is
Got a pocket full of big faces
Throw it up 'cause every nigga that I'm with Taylor

[Chorus:]
Yeah, uh huh, you know what it is
Everything I do, I do it big
Yeah, uh huh screaming that's nothing
What I pulled off the lot, that's stunting
Repping my town when you see me you know everything
Black and yellow [x4]
I put it down from the whip to my diamonds I'm in
Black and yellow [x4]

[Verse 3:]
Stay high like how I'm supposed to do
That crown underneath them clouds, cant get close to you
And my car look unapproachable
Super clean but its super mean

She wanna fuck with them cats, smoke weed, count stacks, get fly, take trips and that's that
Real rap, I let her get high, she wouldn't she feel that, convertible drop fill, 87 the top peel back

[Chorus:]
Yeah, uh huh, you know what it is
Yeah, uh huh, you know what it is
Repping my town when you see me you know everything
Black and yellow [x4]
I put it down from the whip to my diamonds I'm in
Black and yellow [x4]
Yeah, uh huh, you know what it is
Everything I do, I do it big
Yeah, uh huh screaming that's nothing
What I pulled off the lot, that's stunting
Repping my town when you see me you know everything
Black and yellow [x4]
I put it down from the whip to my diamonds I'm in
Black and yellow [x4]

OVER (Drake Featuring Chiggy)

[Chiggy]
I'm far from Over
I mean I'm far from done
So far gone
Drugged up, feeling sleepy on that lithium
Depressed no, but I'm on that Downer shit
Let's get low, ride me slow
Girl don't blow me off, gimme a blow
The trumpets blow
Heaven's calling
She feels she's at the Pearly Gates
Not to sound dumb, but she's about to come
Cloud 9 shit
Mind in a haze, we've been fuckin' for days
Insomniac sex
Little rest after sex
Dick back up when my body grazes her flesh
Guess what's next
A sex song, Drake call me wrong
But niggaz be fucking bitches to this your song
Testy but feisty is my demeanor to lames
No games, I don't play
But I got on playstation just to prove to baby girl I got game.

[Drake - Chorus]
I know way too many people here right now that I didn't know last year
who the fuck are y'all?
I swear it feels like the last few nights we've been everywhere and back
but I just can't remember it all
what am I doing, what am I doing?
oh yeah thats right, I'm doing me, I'm doing me
I'm living life right now man
and this what I'm do 'til it's over
'til it's over, it's far from over

[Verse 1]
alright, bottles on me
long as someone drink it
never drop the ball, fuck y'all thinking
making sure the young money ship is never sinking
bout to set it off in this bitch Jada Pinkett
I shouldn't have drove, tell me how I'm getting home
you too fine to be laying down in bed alone
I can teach you how to speak my language Rosetta stone
I swear this life is like the sweetest thing I've ever known
got to go thriller Mike Jackson on these n'ggas
all I need is a fucking red jackets with some zippers
super good smidoke a package of the swishas
I did it over night, it couldn't happen any quicker
y'all know them, but fuck it me either
but point the biggest skeptic out I'll make them a believer
it wouldn't be the first time I've done it throwing hundreds
when I should be throwing ones bitch I run it ahh

[Chorus]

[Verse 2]
Uhhh,
one thing bout music when it hits you feel no pain
and I swear I got this shit that makes these bitches go insane
so they tell me that they love me I know better than that it's just game
it's just what comes from fame
and I'm ready for that I'm just saying
I really can't complain, everything is kosher
two thumbs up, ebert and roeper
I really can't see the end getting any closer
but I'll probably still be the man when everything is over
so I'm riding through the city with my high beams on
can you see me can you see me get your visine on
y'all just do not fit the picture
turn your widescreen on

if you thinking Imma quit before I die dream on
man they treat me like a legend
am I really this cold
I'm really too young to be feeling this old
it's about time you admit it who you kidding man
nobody's ever done it like I did it
ahh

[Chorus]

ON MY WAY (Chamillionaire Featuring Chiggy)

[Chiggy]

Soon as I hit the stage
Homies feel the rage
So engaged, busy with living
Old soul, now known to act my age
Stage fright ain't a dilemma now
But I'd rather watch than be on stage or the podium
My tragic lyrics leaving casualties
Mics on fire, lame rappers feel haywired
Thinking I'ma get at them
Think I'd act like Semen (sea men)
And curse them out like a Sailor, shit!
I bring storms when I brainstorm
Rain on them hoes, leaving girls wet without money, shit
The Rainman
The Moodiest
My sinuous mind snaking around unpredictably
Nicki minaj's fine ass perturbing my dick's mind
She's real fine
But older like good wine!
I'ma set time just to vibe so baby we can recline
I'm +On My Way+
To make you feel fine or real good
Thinking of you puts my dick on
I mean I get a hard-on when I think lovingly
Of how much I wanna make love to you.

[Chamillionaire feat. Lee-Lonn)

On my way... my way... mmmm yeah
On my way... my way...

You just need motivation
So I'm thinking you should let me give you more the conversation
Just a demonstration how I'm a lay your body down
I am on my way I'm in my ride I am costing headed to you
I am on my, my way mmmm
In my ride and I am costing headed to you
I am on my way, my way
Take it easy

When I'm pulling up in my drive miss
You know is normally topless
You know these suckers they ain't got this
Cause they car garages is are drop less
I hope your door is unlocked if you need I be your new locksmith
I took so long cause my driveway is like a parking lot at metropolis
I'm always care for which whip to choose
No evidence for getting choose if breaking bars was against the rules
I know every day I will be getting sued
Chop the screwed to get you in the mood
Get out your shoes and get in the nude
Ever since they told me money talks
I have been chatting like I am getting interviewed
It must be something that is in my scoto
That makes a model to say that she swallow
On the way all and I can say is I'm there before you done with the bottle
Shift the gear then now hit the throttle I swerve so much that I missed the pothole
One the way it's your lucky day I'm about to make you feel
Like you hit the lotto

[Chorus:]
You just need motivation
So I'm thinking you should let me give you more the conversation
Just a demonstration how I'm a lay your body down
I am on my way I'm in my ride I am costing headed to you
I am on my, my way
In my ride and I am costing headed to you
I am on my way, my way
Take it easy

I turn the corner I'm a tip it down
You in the presents of greatness
Never been a chef boyardee I can't let the women in cake mix
That's Tasteless and I taste chips
Forget the the kid for my lateness before you even turn off the lights
I be there to give you that face lift
What I meant by that last line is that
I'm a be in your face like botox
If you got socks then lose those socks

And have nothing on but your broke box
Diamonds larger than road rocks
While I'm trying to prove how to show stop
Car looking like a cruse ship I got no garage
I load docks (I load docks)
No road blocks (no road blocks)
I flow daily (I flow daily)
And you'll flow too When I ge to you It'll get so wavy
I'm the only player who you know lately then can coach a girl
To get so crazy make her kiss a girl like you know Caitie
I can motivate you let's go baby

[Chorus:]
You just need motivation
So I'm thinking you should let me give you more the conversation
Just a demonstration how I'm a lay your body down
I am on my way I'm in my ride I am costing headed to you
I am on my, my way
In my ride and I am costing headed to you
I am on my way, my way
Take it easy

I'm about to exit the freeway to break you off if you let me
I just know that you let me
I just know that you let me
I am pulling up in your drive way I just hope that you're ready
I just hope that you're ready
I just hope that you're ready
Nothing but the finest candy coats is what you're tasting
Push it to the limit call it motor motivation
Hope you're buckled up I hope your seat belt got you're braced in
Texas player so will do but slow will switch the paced in

I'll be the player headed to your location
And be the person that you put in your faith in
The pillow that you let you know waiting
Will be the pillow that you put your face in
I told her never get must aching
I know I'm better than the rest I got great win
Good thanks, but those who stay patient I bet a get a couple standing ovation

[Chorus:]
You just need motivation
So I'm thinking you should let me give you more the conversation
Just a demonstration how I'm a lay your body down
I am on my way I'm in my ride I am costing headed to you
I am on my, my way
In my ride and I am costing headed to you

I am on my way, my way
Take it easy

****